A Landscaped Garden
for the Addict

A Landscaped Garden
for the Addict

poems by

Judith Skillman

SHANTI ARTS PUBLISHING
BRUNSWICK, MAINE

A Landscaped Garden for the Addict

Published by Shanti Arts Publishing
Interior and cover design by Shanti Arts Designs

Cover image by Egon Schiele (1890–1918), *Field of Flowers*, 1910. Chalk, pastel, gouache, and gold paint on paper. Wikimedia Commons. Public Domain.

Shanti Arts LLC
193 Hillside Road
Brunswick, Maine 04011
shantiarts.com

Printed in the United States of America

ISBN: 978-1-951651-99-2 (softcover)

Library of Congress Control Number: 2021944634

for my daughter Jocelyn Skillman, a true healer

Other Titles by Judith Skillman

Oscar the Misanthropist, Floating Bridge Press, 2021

The Truth about Our American Births, Shanti Arts Publishing, 2020

Came Home to Winter, Deerbrook Editions, 2019

Premise of Light, Tebot Bach, 2018

Kafka's Shadow, Deerbrook Editions, 2017

Angles of Separation, Glass Lyre Press, 2015

House of Burnt Offerings, Pleasure Boat Studio, 2014

The Phoenix: New & Selected Poems, Dream Horse Press, 2014

Broken Lines—The Art and Craft of Poetry, Lummox Press 2013

The White Cypress, Červená Barva Press, 2011

The Never, Dream Horse Press, 2010

Prisoner of the Swifts, Ahadada Books, 2009

Heat Lightning: New and Selected Poems, Silverfish Review Press, 2006

Circe's Island, Silverfish Review Press, 2003

Red Town, Silverfish Review Press, 2001

Storm, Blue Begonia Press, 1998

Beethoven and the Birds, Blue Begonia Press, 1996

Worship of the Visible Spectrum, Breitenbush Books, 1988

"I cannot but conclude that the Bulk of your Natives,
to be the most pernicious Race of little odious Vermin
that Nature ever suffered to crawl
upon the Surface of the Earth."

—Jonathan Swift, *Gulliver's Travels*

Contents

────────────── **FOUR** ──────────────

────────────── **FIVE** ──────────────

Acknowledgements

Thanks to the editors of the following journals and anthologies where these poems first appeared:

Artemis: "Stricture of Pain" and "Veils"

Breath and Shadow: "Chronicle" and "Come this way, he said, and I followed him"

Cimarron Review: "Testimonial"

Curiouser Magazine: "Milfoil"

Ghazal Page: "Your Grandmother"

Hubbub: "The Dog House"

Journal of the American Medical Association (JAMA): "Bone Weary"

Lights, Pleasure Boat Press: "A July of Julys" and "Long Marriage Prayer"

Linden Avenue Literary Journal: "Below the Snow Line"

Pangyrus: "Short History of the Accident"

Piltdown Review: "Bric-a-Brac"

New Reader Magazine: "Doubt"

Silkworm: "The Cold Descends"

Sou'wester: "The Yeoman"

Terror House Magazine: "Treatise" and "To My God in His Affliction"

The Hartskill Review: "Written While Possessed of a Gulliverian Myopia"

The Mom Egg: "Clover" and "Wintering Over"

The Nashville Review: "Wintering Over"

The Poeming Pigeon: "No, It's Called Flower"

The Selkie: "A Long Convalescence"

The Stickman Review: "Raindrops"

What Rough Beast, Indolent Press: "Crow the Only Constant," "From Your Own Filthy Mouth," "Time as Infection," and "Fear and Trembling"

"Scarlet Tanagers" is reprinted from *The Ending Hasn't Happened Yet*, Sable Books

"October" is reprinted from Futures Anthology, Bell Press

"Low Dose Opioid Hyperalgesia" previously appeared as "Hyperalgesia" in *Premise of Light*, Tebot Bach, 2019. Thanks to Mifanwy Kaiser for permission to reprint.

With gratitude to my colleagues in writing and the arts: Janée J Baugher, Christianne Balk, Sharon Hashimoto, Carol Kelly, Tina Kelly, Susan Lane, Linera Lucas, Kurt Olsson, Anne Pitkin, Michael Spence, Diane Ray, Joannie Stangeland, Mary Ellen Talley, Ruthie V., and Lillo Way.

Thanks to my mother, Dr. Bernice Bloom Kastner, for her unstinting support.

ONE

The Yeoman

Tells me to walk in a circle
beside his ox. For each step
I take the brand will sear me—
he holds the hot poker.

The hole inside grows larger
with his prod. I do as I am
told. Soon the moon,
a kind of low grade fever,
breaks through blackberry bushes
along the edge of undreamt rashes.

The yeoman governs his small
landed estate, of which I am become
part—my hips for the use of man,
my belly for bearing, and my back
a surgeon broke to stretch—
broke to stretch into a long line
of mothers. I walk and yelp
the generation's generational dance.

From Your Own Filthy Mouth

Come curses, cries of the medievalist's
rack stuck up your spine, waiting to pull
you into another form. Grandmother?
Daughter? Girl who had the knife flashed at her

in hallways of the first interracial school?
You hear a fish spit into a toilet,
see the adze in the mirror hung over
a row of off-white porcelain sinks.

You turn to let out a belch from inside the whale,
you weep against the walls
of an obsidian belly
where once a tiny maggot bred

from sperm and egg performed meiosis.
Sway on a stalk, usher in another
smooth-skinned creature for whom
you'll perform the rites of spring, old mother f'er.

Crow the Only Constant

Dogs three eagles, harasses, caws,
asks to be forgiven its murderous rages,
blackens the corner of your eyes,
stamps out the last passion
you had for your lover.

Crow flies as it flies—
no measurement
captures feathers, no short cut
from one surgery to the next,
for bone graft taken from iliac joint of the hip.

Crow walks like a Rabbi in the streets, *hop hop.*
Climb on board—the next train
leaves for your trial,
the one you will lose to the persecutors
and the maggots that dwell

in the lily of your arm.
From a square of cornflower sky
comes crow's petulance—
a barrage of hoarse cries,
rages and tantrums of a June baby.

A Long Convalescence

It is the small things tell you you are home—
cotton sheets, linen clouds, Dutch rabbits
nibbling greens. It is close to sunset
when you remember why you went away.
Never again, I swear on the Bible
I hear you say to yourself as if no one
heard you. Mama hurries the last crumbs
into a basket, sister sings her song.
However many hours He wore that crown—
that's how long you lay anesthetized
while the surgeon scraped nerves and stretched bones.
Meanwhile the jackrabbit comes to blend in
against tan grounds and cottonwood. Windows
hold a million trees full of ganglia.
Accept that for now you will be going
between only two rooms—one with a bed,
one with a sink. Its grave porcelain eye.

October

Slant light comes now to tell
of whorls. The sky leafs in
in yellow clouds, the fence
jaunty. When you waken
at dawn the late bird sings
from its thicket of change.

Beneath the ground roots blue,
put down spikes for water's
return. You stitched your all
to summer's long hot days,
lost a border, knew youth.

Why pin the dying seeds
to their grasses when milk-
weed gives up its wishes
to rejoice in harsh winds?

All's askew—the day, the
hour in this your sister's
birthday month. You pine for
the limelight, instead re-
ceive the applause of a-
corns falling on wooden
decks, and diagnoses.

Scarlet Tanagers

Climbing branches of fir.
Spots of color
on a soft, quiet, gray day.
It could be a birthday.

The dream where her legs
lie in a shallow pool
and she can't pull herself
up the ledge

to join the others on the patio.
The deadweight of a paralysis
she narrowly escaped,
reflected years later

as annular tears
fixed to facet joints
in her lumbar spine.
All dreams rooted

like the tree these birds
disappear from
carrying strokes of cad red,
expensive and rare.

Stricture of Pain

In hot or cold lands equally abundant,
given freely to the body as it ages,
nerves as delicate as flower petals,
skin thinned down to the last pink layers.

Walk slowed to syrup, and the first leaves
drifting down to embroider the lie
of any paradise whatsoever,
the bobcat's fearless predation over

rabbits, the starless sky. In every life
the same tale—unless, heroic—we die young.
Otherwise we drink the draught offered, cupped

in veined hands, either mimicking Polly-
anna or growing more bitter with each
morning's summons to leave the womb called *bed*.

The Dog House

In here again, head rubbing the ceiling
like another Alice who drank the wrong potion,
took too many pills of different colors,

I can feel with legs, my belly,
and the stoop in my back,
how long it will be before I'm let out

to breathe the pure scents of spring.
In here with nothing but that smell
of old carpet, sheets never washed,

the scrappy ball in a corner, I feel
yellow with age. A sepia print of myself,
and the guilt-stamps I collected

arrayed like tattoos across my chest,
where boobs hang. Once they were called
a rack. I call them boobs because I'm bad—

bad sleep, bad breath, bad with almost
everything I do. Befriending my owner—
how's that good? Playing fetch—

in what fashion
does it secure the surety of plenty?
Once I had a cornucopia of gifts,

and, puppy-like, others admired the place
I occupied in the world. They stared,
admired, openly seduced. The lake

seemed big when we'd row across
to the other side, where chalk cliffs
rose and time stretched like string

in water so clear you could lap it up
and it would never taint. *Those days
are gone*—a phrase so trite I say it

in my dog voice. I practice saying it
over and over again, watching
ants wander the dirt floor. Cold

seeps in, the sun clips the horizon
doing what it always does, which is to say,
going down, as I sigh again, repulsed

by my own doggedness, my desire
to please, hating, as I settle in
for the long haul, this night where stars

glitter. Treats I had but couldn't keep,
jewels so obdurate they only exist
even now many light years away.

Lurid Spring

Another spate of ornamentals—
flower after fruitless flower,
sprig after sprig of currant,
plum, and cherry. Verdant sword ferns.
Here the two lovers walk uphill.
She turns to kiss him, her blonde braid
like Gretel's. He's handsome as Hansel
and hardy enough. They cross
one of many wooden bridges
over three sets of falls.
Lovers set against the earth in March,
light as robins who seek the worm
without seeing their own orange
breasts. Youths fraudulent
and fat enough to feed the flames
or be the fodder.

Bric-a-Brac

Outside, the barber pole, a swirl
of symbolic spirals, and walk
upstairs, touching, as you go,
the *espagnolette*, which gives purchase
to your hand, opening inward
where the first *bijou* gleams like a clue
on a map that leads to the tiny globe
set in a stand so the hand can spin
a journey for the body to walk
between statuary, statue, and statuettes.
One giraffe taller than the *jardinière's*
placed just inside the doorway,
where chimes announce a visitor
as the cuckoo clucks its hour.

Onward, then, in pilgrimage
toward walls on which sprays,
sconces, swags, fold their velvet creases
toward the sun you crave in blinded
spigots, and become aware
of the grandfather clock, the *girandole*
upon whose five stars wax beaded,
held the shape of the last supper.
Farther then, into the walk-through,
where all manner of salver make you
salivate, though you're barely able
to enter this kitchen without breaking a *tazza*.

Call it ornament, nonetheless
cuspidation's been at work here
with its lures, *objets trouvés*, and *patens*.
Menorah, *modillion*, and *monteith*

conspire to fill each space with *bibelots*,
non-alcoholic punch the latter's
last drink, and, continue inward, your eyes
see patterns, kaleidoscopic, pontypooled
now from fatigue of many nights spent
awake in this elaborate house,
several diptychs open, too many trinkets
offering up to sight a sense of curios.

And then the single crucifix,
round which vermiculation troubles
background. So far the journey
into a place of decoration remains
gilded more than guild, until you realize
this flat represents an age.

The tiny piano holds its smile,
the triptych's no more three dimensional
than the diptych's two, and no, nothing
blesses you in ultima. It's simply suggestion—
the serving of yellowed beverages,
the hallway littered with collections
from antiquity when you began to leave
bizarre calling cards on the shelf
beside that speculum in the foyer.

There, an antique door's French panes,
changed from glass to mirrors, where—
you?—your face?—gone from flesh
to *quatrefoil* hangs, the hangdog look of an elder,
a random personage of no great value, in that
you—(do you see?) have come three flights up
to worship horizontals.

TWO

Bone Weary

I can almost taste the shades of gray
rising in layers outside my window.
I still hear the white noise of rain punctured
by the train coming on twin rails way off
in the distance, where others dress

in bright colors for travel. The boundary
between salt water and fresh water,
put in place so long ago it's become
a spit, a sea wall, a piece of land
that no longer troubles me, lies indifferent

as a sponge—its sand compacted, yellow.
They say I am hollow, my nerves shot.
They bring mineral waters. How can I tell
them the infinitely many ways
I struggle to fill the hills and valleys

of a simple conversation? How
make peace with long silences
following on the heels of argument?
I know now that cloth full of smelling salts—
spirit of Hartshorne, eucalyptus oil—

brought me to when I fainted. My walls
clammy, the small dirty room in *greyout*.
I hear sirens. They fill the whittled
semblance of days and nights. I cover
my ears with down pillows.

Taunted

Out past the poorest shacks,
where tricycle and fuel can sit together,
and chairs are stacked for no one's throne,
I walked into insect sounds.
They sweep up my past,
poor as that, and an ironing board
where the isosceles triangle lived.
I walked without you.
Near the river a pair of birds—
brightly colored male,
female neutral to better camouflage
her young. I remembered little wheels
turning a circle of seasons,
hand-me-down clothes,
madras, cigar smoke rings,
the magical realism of childhood.
Out past the edge of town,
where doubt intersects
with luck, and the barrel's bottom—
scraped back to wood—echoes,
I picked a few wildflowers
and longed for the poppy,
well bred, on a schedule.
In my ears the hammer of wear
hits its nail. Dull knife, fork with bent tines,
I'll come back for more of the same
even as these dwellers
off Broadway and Main
return to eat leftovers from off-white plates.

Below the Snow Line

The maid wields her duster. She
Wears the little apron you love to watch,
The one that bares her thighs.
She is meticulous, and young, too young
For such difficult work—keeping
Each and every flake of snow from the needles
Of trees called Evergreen. She smells
Of Paper whites, calls out your name
In a husky, Aussie accent—are you home?
Have you arrived back from the office,
Mission, dock, island, market where you
Picked up a crusty bread and a bottle of white,
Some cheese aged perfectly, the texture
Encaustic as if hot wax were *Brie* and we
Could each bite into our portion of the painting,
Savor the light shining as if from behind.
My hair a halo, yours a ponytail.
You not even interested in her wiles: flirtatious
Backbends as she continually moves lower
And lower and lower.

Finally Silenced

The violin, its slender formula
of song untended,
begins to belong to a case.
Unctuous birds pronounce
the longest day will end.

Where are those suitors
who lingered for years
beneath windows carved
in castle walls? Is there
room for chivalry

in a songless world?
Ask the metal bit
with its chain, fastened
to domesticate a two-ton animal.
What's chewed down to the nub

is blood-breeding,
fly-drawing. Ask those dumb
animals flexing a muscle
as if to soothe
the itch and burn.

To come full circle
means nothing less than suffrage—
lack of redemption
for those who would appropriate
the feminine figure as a symbol.

Short History of the Accident

Each morning the same skull fracture, an indented line I trace
with my fingers in the shower while washing my hair.

The drunk leaning over, telling me it would be OK as I screamed
my son's name.

His flannel shirt and his breath to which I return decades later.

This intention, reader, to procrastinate against pain—we share that—
knowing all that must be gotten through in the palimpsests of age.

No rain, clear night, 7 p.m., a two-year-old's Lego motorcycle
lands upside down beside a drain in the five-lane street.

Rushed to settlement, told it was my fault on account of the boot.

Told jay walking.

For the sake of amnesia I bend again to pick up the boot one size
too large caring only whether or not this little story about my son
remains alive.

Low Dose Opioid Hyperalgesia

They gave me pills for pain
and I took them for my memories,
knowing this taking
carried warnings of dependence.

I became the drug of sleep
slowly, *Hypnos* a mask to cover
amnesia. Afraid to wake
too much I watched birds slip

from trees, heard wind and water
narrow the spaces. Between proverbs
the sun came and went. At times
the moon sprouted like an eye

in the back yard—sinister,
unyielding, veiled by wisps of cloud.
They gave and I took for twenty years
what turned me into this churl

who lives close to the ground.
Instead of fresh blood, my veins
fill with grubs and maggots,
those I recognize as kin

to twinned states of jealousy
and servitude. The little power
I wield comes from restraint.
My drum's grown hollow

as a chimney the woodpecker
hammers in spring.

Ivy

Crosses brick, goes underground,
comes up for air
in the thirsty garden,
its leaf mimetic,
sharp, a pattern I recall
like music.

Garter snakes molt
between the cracks
in the blacktop.
An old military installation,
radio towers pierce
white skies.

My hidden life—
I have to pull it up,
come clean
for the sake of decorum.
Then comes trauma.
At the core it reeks

of sentiment.
The root struggles
against my hand. For every scrap
of ground I gain
I give away another self.
Can a flower be brown?

Can an organ deviate
from the norm?
In the March weeds
I see portents, anomalous hearts
looped together,
fringed with longing.

Your Grandmother

Older than drear, in pain from stooping and bending
over to lead you towards the table, still she's bent

on having gourds and candles, she's gesturing, bent
at the crook of the age, the season. Trees are bending

at your feet as if praying. Blue jays call. All eyes suspend
their disbelief at your skin soft as a plum, your rending

cries when hurt. In many ways your grandmother's bending
towards you now for that short span before the road bends

and takes her from this little play of listing, carrying, and bending
into the clear-sighted view of youth. Listen, unbending

one, free your grandmother from the burdens of bending.
Take these thick stitches cast on by decades, calcified bendings

of aorta, disc, and tissue. Where the juncture captures and bends
her loose into memory, cast off into summer, bending

round to see a little boatful of gourds and candles sending
her ashes into a lake. Don't let them fool you as you bend

down on your knees. She heard *plane, bird, ask.* Bending
over to hear your battle cry became her best heart's rending.

Written While Possessed of a Gulliverian Myopia

To see the hairs stand out
on a miniature Thistle
wedded to cactus stalk.
To see dust on a Leaf of the orchid
hunched in one corner for lack
of sustenance, to want to pull
out a Cloth and clean
the fat green paddle stuck out,
flowerless for one year
that turned into two.
Air roots gesturing like the Arms
of a Drowning man.

To be Exquisitely sensitive
to the Touch of my Master,
who strokes me with his Thumb
when I discourse upon
our Country's constitution—
tales of truth-telling, of Adjudications
passed down fairly, which he mistakes
for attempts at justification.

To have to Wear my size
and live in a shoebox, and then
to have shat in his Hand.

Or this, a telling example
of Predicament foisted
upon the Innocent person
who stumbles into a Land
unrecognizable from home.

I wear the Overalls, I trek
the hanging bridge. It swings
in winds so strong they'd snap
the Firs, and yellow wood
spill its ochre mush-wood
beneath the same Sun
that shines still beneath a sky
I don't Remember leaving.
Its Dome-like qualities
reigned in the unknown.
This bridge spans a Crevasse
I recognize from nightmare—the one
all my People have. Inheritance
blessed us with a Negligible amount
of Introversion spiced with notes
of autism, the need for Chocolate
and Distaste for wine.

Perhaps this is a thick place,
I will try to feed it
with as many Tiny chickens
as my pockets hold. And from
the left one, after crossing
through this nomenclature called text,
A kind of gibberish to His Majesty.

I pull out a Hen, and gulping it
down whole, Recall, as I swallow,
the familiar picture, learned
from anatomy Encyclopedias,
where a Single plastic sheet placed
over another, repeated for Sets
of muscles, organs, bones, etc.,
revealed the Human body

to be simply a Machine—
a tube containing, among other
inner hallways, two pipes.

One for air and one for food.
Their Openings placed so close
my mother (may God Bless her soul)
often Choked on the Cornish,
its tiny claws tickling her windpipe
when I Spoke to her.

Wintering Over

We know the cold, the lack.
We feel the sun crammed
          into its thimble
in a corner of sky.

          Abandoned
as by a lover, we've rehearsed
the lake's absent color,
sunset and stick trees.

When we were children
sent to bed without supper,
          our faces
burned from being slapped.

If it weren't for shame,
          our cheeks
would be pale
as unblanched almonds.

Our debts piled high,
we leave the house
          to stake
what's left on a horse,
a bolt of silk,
a sweater
of loose holes, and no buttons.

Time as Infection

Past and future beckon forward, backward,
take the gray dust of years, plow it under.
Before bed you become old. While downstairs
it could be yesterday, upstairs flights become
tomorrow. Nowhere does the *now* flourish.
The present's undernourished—a runt coyote,
a spindly animal too young to count,
too yellow not to fear. Hunger in those

red eyes, the glint of an inhuman hide
poised to take what it needs, just as you did.
For that you've suffered. Galileo, forced
into house arrest, said *sotto voce,*
Nonetheless, the earth moves around the sun.
When did history become your life?

THREE

A Landscaped Garden for the Addict

While I turned the earth upside down
and cut back the juniper's arms,
those dead arteries of wood,
I thought of you
in your late-morning bed of dreams.

I walked around the Japanese maple,
picked up the thread of light
dances there sometimes and turns the world
green. Saw desire rising in the hardy fuchsia,
its red bells and crimson half moons
moving slightly in the breeze,
making morning seem like evening.
The air glittered with overheard telephone conversations
and spiders who amassed their silken avenues,
their chances to connect.

Now I imagine your chin
dropped to your chest, and you
taken in again by the poppy,
every nerve-ending waving in unison
as if to say *it is a far distance to paradise*
but we may yet arrive.

The grass grows ragged around
the little semblance of order I have reclaimed
but you are brilliant in your craving
for only the heart of the flower
as you fall further into those sleeves of dark
which the high has bought for itself.

If I Were Gulliver

The world's huge, especially turkeys
and all the work accompanying that syringe
used for basting. There's no getting around
degenerative discs. The grass greens
each November regardless in weather
so wet and cold one hates to compete with it.

On the other hand, at least the idea
of being small's become reasonable. At first
it had an exile quality to it—being from
a different country, having parents that didn't fit in.

I saw my mother's hands slathered with grease
as she broke bone from flesh, and how each carrot
fell into place in her famous soups—who knew
what a quandary for my obsessive compulsive cleaning.
I followed her around with Windex, wiping
each handle pulled by her lubed hands,
feeling oppressed by the largesse of Thanksgiving.

And still, the world's too big for me to find
a tiny watercolor where I can climb into a sailboat
and ride around. No one brings me a menu
filled with petit fours. Each meal includes dicing.
hand-washing, high cabinets filled with plates
one must have, filigreed cups out of reach.
The sky late afternoon turning blue-gray.

Carbon, soot, oxides—that's my mind in a Heimlich
as I gallantly try to re-program the zones
where highways to pain, originally paved
in the eighties, continue to put out Light speed signals,

received. *Miniscule Synapse*: if I had a dog
that would be his name, or *MS* for short.
It's a nice day, the neighbors would say
as I sat in a recliner in my shoebox, in the diorama
with the plaque over the fireplace:
"There's No Place Like Home."

Lost

What does it mean when you dream you are lost?
That there's a witch who will come and find you,
Poke a stick through a chink in the prison
Of what's left of your longing for change?

Or that the road will stretch, yawn, widen
Before you, your car swerve into another
And the man in that car smile politely
As he nicks a bit of your ego, and flakes fall like snow
In the soundless state you thought you had forgotten?

Does it mean you're a child again, rocking back and forth
In the back seat, watching the moon follow
Every turn and twist in the highway?

When you're lost, the parents take you back
As if you were still precious,
Wrapping the dysfunction of their arms
Around the small, cold back of your child-self,
Taking your miniature face in their wolfish hands
And peering into the sockets of your eyes
As if they could read every thought you'd ever thought.

Treatise

You could say cottonwood falls to earth.
You might say the white fluff contains catkins.
Neither of these statements is wrong. They miss
the point, which is that cottonwood
makes a crevice, an outline, signals

the end of May, the beginning
of a summer always come too soon
to allow happiness, pleasure, comfort.
Driven here and there by wind, a blizzard
for those unnerved, inarticulate hungers.

Number the trees along the boulevard.
You could say softness, like sex, is a thing
of the past. Perhaps your face caves in,
your eyelashes shorten beneath the gaze
of a German optometrist who would

explain propagation as a matter
of numbers. Irrational to the end,
these wishes still enter through sliders,
accompany you in the car, stick
to light sweaters. *May you be well,* a friend

writes, thinking to cheer you up.
Whether the seeds rise or fall
sickness has taken root in your sleep.
The architecture's ruined. For proof, stage 4
doubles as dreamtime. How can you rescue

the other, lighter woman, the one
who was drowned by a mask in order
to save two lives? Her infant grew beyond
the hospital and left mama behind
to fend off these intrusive peddlers.

Music in the Gutter

Only there, collecting its parts,
the rusty oboe, clarinet,
violin from a pawn shop—
one whose bridge has fallen
and strings lie like ribbons
against yellow wood.

Trickling and rising, falling
and stopping against needles
from the great Sequoia—
the song of Vitali's
infinite sadness,
of Beethoven's buzzing ears.

Farther away a car leeches
oil from the street.
A plane scratches the sky.
I alone do not possess the wherewithal
to lift myself into the music
Father began, and which

continues apace with or without
the consent of my fingers.
Only for me the fate of listener—
for I possess a rarified Gramophone
in which each of God's sounds
is, sadly, magnified.

Too bad you have not heard
in the rain those fingers
of a lecherous man—
the dusty cradles once held dolls
who could not be born,
infinitely small and cracked fetuses.

Raindrops

Singletons foolhardy enough to come in two,
in sets, ghosts notes foolhardy as to be seen—
long stripes the rainbow left when it disappeared.
Nation of water and excess, each little drill another source
of loss and discontent. Or else what music calls
to the earth from its dislocated sky, low-hanging, pregnant
with Noah's flood. Again inundated, as in dream.
A slow truth brings the body back—it is the other
who lies between two worlds. It is the uncle shrunken to half
his size, that one who succored me with smoke rings
from his ear. Child, the birdbath fills, come, let us drink.

As Before Sickness

The fabric of infection—
　　　　how well it absorbs sound.
In a fever a thousand lifetimes.

Like silk organza, how delicate the skin
　　　　though we pretend
to be headstrong little women.

Instead of confidence
　　　　oh Mary fetch a pail,
we remember what it is the cherubim left

when their wings broke,
　　　　when they stroked the air
with the hot breath of peppers.

A nostalgic rain comes to the garden. Mother
　　　　returns to the kitchen to make toast.
Blue glass objects line the sill—

bottles, cups, neck of Rilke's swan . .
　　　　They'd left their childhood.
Even the stove with its open-mouthed darkness,

its velvet fingerlings of heat
　　　　inclines toward the saying
of omens and portents.

My Anguish

When the deer
come to graze
early morning, and fall to their
knees
to take their short sleep—
it is like that,
always vigilant
waiting to be found and shot
in an open field
the sun has stained brown.

Where the road comes to a *t*
and one must choose
left or right
after driving many hours away
from bad dreams—
it is like that,
forever unable to reverse
what happened
on the wrong side of fate.

Why the men play at war
as if immortal, placing
between them each evening
the children—
it is like that, based on the body,
married to the premise
of a horizontal world,
its blood-red horizon
coated in soot and flames.

Imprimatura

Hooded bird, come in,
convalesce, hold conversation
with the unknown speaker.
Me, me, me, chirps the sparrow
through an open window.

On railings other would-be wishers
of gladness gather.
Crow, you come too,
dominate with shadow
the tabula rasa of sickness.

Who gets sick?
The sick get sick.
Cloud, rag, turpentine,
chloroform, influenza—
a table set with a vase of fruit.

Orator, forehead of a Latin speaker
placed upside down—
lift the cloak of illness,
its spell begun in a home
called *pig sty.*

Come this way, he said, and I followed him

through a clearing, along a well-worn path
to avoid descending large lava rocks

we would have to switchback our way down.
Basalt so slippery a misstep could mean
a broken ankle. I didn't question the word

short cut. It meant a kind of reprieve from,
a nuanced name for the kind of invalid
I'd become, one who couldn't, even with hiking

boots, climb down a hill alone. A Jill
who would come tumbling after, a Jack
who'd hold my hand, steady my body

against his own, navigate terrain once
ocean floor: *pillow basalt*. Where before
we'd slowly and steadily seen the town

come into focus—its churched roofs and alleys,
Peoh Point on the other side, the sky
emblazoned with the same sun as always

only hotter—this time we would bypass
any chance of lost footing by continuing on.
Short was good, short meant shorter.

Instead the trail grew down and up terrain
engineered for bikes and horses, through
birch and alder; alder and fir, on until

even without my saying he knew how tiring
the weight of pain in hip and sacrum, bulging
discs—this appendage called body—he knew

a little less than before about why
and how difficult a simple August day
away from home could be. As far

as we'd come, I felt the sweating trees,
and thirsted for the end of things, though
perhaps he didn't know that much, how pain

changes a person, wrapped like ivy
or morning glory around the cord called *spine*.
The story never ends, it goes on

even now that short cut's become a joke
between us, one he uses affectionately,
as if to tell me it doesn't matter

how long the thing will hold out—infra-
structure of what never had nerves before,
walking upright, walking, walking onward

into the state we call unknown, our not
having a map of the future perhaps
enough to keep the road to home whole.

FOUR

Long Marriage Prayer

The lichen and the lichen's kin.
Rabbits black and black and white

sun themselves on winter days.
The dirt road leads to a tenement

where a man and a woman live
to peel back the skin of one

another until inside the core
the self's cut loose to fester and burn.

Do onion tears sting? The lichen
gray on green, the evening lengthening.

I wish for a crust of armor,
for stars on snow. I want

to hear the tinkle of snowmelt
and know that you left first.

Cold Snap

Morning of old snow.
I sit in the declension of waking
or being woken.
Sparkles of sun star grounds
blued with shadows.

On the statue of Hera in Berlin
broken arms belie nobility,
the missing head
and strong thighs tell of anger.
All jealousy's more than plaster.

In this postcard the trees don't move.
The sun in its castle-sky
casts long trunks across hillocks
where the cloven-hooved ones step,
looking for grasses.

Doubt

I like to drink the ink.
It was all much better then.
In the greenbelt, with a comrade or two.

Walking in snow, hearing the crunch
beneath our boots as stars ground the sky
toward another bone-tinged dawn. Sleep?
Not on our watch. Dreams?

We didn't need them. We lived
with our daemons. Their hunger
fed on three squares.

I like to chew the wee hour
until it howls. Like the Northwest coyote
they put down, the one who lingered
near the golf course.

That animal wasn't afraid
of the human.
Liked the taste of dog and cat.

I like to entertain the certain death
that is my own—
pure in its salt-sure,
half-witted visions of heaven.

The Invalid

I come to her in the evening
when the earth has cooled
and gracious plants bow their heads
to the grass.

Her face a doppelgänger,
her terrors born of fever dreams.
I make her comfortable
in the room of my childhood,

a cinderblock barrack
with cement floors.
We sleep in one bed,
like Irish twins.

I crush an aspirin between spoons
and add sugar and juice.
When I stand
at the edges of her disappearance

the room has a taste,
though it's been papered
with a skin of new wallpaper.
Japanese pagodas and whisper-flowers.

Julio returns from the morgue,
his face gone white
from making the identification.
She was killed at nine

on her pink bicycle,
sucked under a truck

on a Montreal boulevard.
I come to her every September.

How long before these Siamese
are separated? Will her nails
be painted in the nacre
of a common shell?

A July of Julys

Heat on glass, the shifting begins.
Houses rise to ten degrees
above air temperature,
doors swell in their frames.

War contains no people,
only images. Those who live
on browning earth,
landlocked, have nowhere to go.

Nomads bear no children.
Tots with big brown eyes
like deer—already sacrificed
on Agamemnon's altar.

Outside, inside
remain countries apart.
Fire burns in the heart,
blood boils. Pretend water

never existed except in the mouth
of the crocodile, slots
of the sprinkler, scream
of the kettle.

The Cold Descends

From a sky of Payne's gray
hail stones collect on a patio.
Inside a clutch of women rise from their chairs,
open a sliding door, reach out their hands

for wadded notes of lovers,
robin's egg blue eggs of robins,
frivolous wine charms,
stuffing of dolls and animals.

Because not one rabbit will be born
in the winter, the women have begun to laugh
as when they were young
and the tides ruled their bodies.

Their sides split as they reach out
from Irene's house of lentil soup
to catch that bit of ice
that could save them from their age.

Of Lichen

Here in timberland
it's the same old game
of algae and symbiosis,
co-dependency.

Sleep the commodity
one can't get without a benzo.
Short term memory impaired.

Is it snow or moonlight?
Was the snow here
all day today
or has it newly fallen?

Chronicle

And have you struggled against the pain
as if stretched on a Procrustean bed,
and did the morning find you here again?

Was there nothing, neither sun nor rain,
to restore the lithe, gymnastic spine
and have you struggled against the pain?

Lone women done with children, complain
to yourselves about the children's children.
The next morning finds you here again.

Spurred vertebrae leak lamina, strain
against gravity's hearty grip. Discs drip.
And have you struggled against the pain?

Go tint your cheeks with delicate paint
after a mandatory hot shower.
And have you struggled against the pain,
and did the morning find you here again?

This Close

Yet you stay away
how many days
as the moon swells
from crescent to half
to full. I remain
behind, watching you
swell and puff
like an adder snake
or a rattler, wanting
to leave, not knowing
how the knot
untied its ribbon.
I am refused—
your forked tongue
(your slit pupil)
daily drags me
through the canyon
of our marriage.

Fragment

Downstairs the washer churns,
outside sun sears a dun lawn.
This pain is not Dickinson's,
it belongs to me. She has her hope—
I my synaptic fault.

Does a tiger clings to forms
that no longer exist?
This stenosis in my body
is a sign that it visits others
at the home, the market, the fêtes.

Yes, the server in this Home
know the habits of disease
as she makes her rounds,
saving a bit of soup from the kitchen
to eat on break from a small white bowl.

No, It's Called Flower

Not weed, I was told
by the young man
behind the counter.
Weed is seen in a bad light,
he explained, *for its connotations.*

Flower—here he gestured
at thick buds of Kush,
Strawberry Pie, and Diesel
filling glass jars,
spilling their scent

into the room, arrayed
in shades of verdant green,
huge buds horny as hell
for what they'd been deprived of.
—*Flower is pretty, more acceptable.*

I applaud your rebranding,
I said, the question
of how to inhale
without burning my throat
still there on my lips, unasked.

FIVE

Veils

We've reached the other-world. Wisps of cloud
hang like shawls over the mountains. Leaves
turn red. Where the bridge hangs rust grows out
from rock, burgeoning.

There is no place
left for God. All day the peaks rose and fell
until, at night we found a bar where those
who tend snow gather to tell stories.

In one a boy who was our son careened
into an abyss of ice. In another
the girl who was our daughter fell and rode
beneath her horse, dragged by a rope.

It's all the same weather,
smoke or mist, a swath cut in tall grass
where deer once wandered towards berries,
the Padma of Vishnu.

Please don't forget
to honor our dead, to arm your sadness
with a lotus flower, a conch, a mace,
a discus. The cover up's a *fait
accompli*. Children are always involved—
children and secrets, envelopes and whiteness.

Thinking of Limes in the North

The man's changed again, suddenly, fuse
lit by a scent come into a leaf
so succulent he must've wanted
to eat it whole, and go from there
into the center of the bush, pulling

under ripe fruit with his teeth,
hearing the sound a lime makes
when it comes off its sprocket
above a canyon marked by interstates
crossing and recrossing what was once

the floor of a great ocean.
Ever since she saw the number of green citrus
held like tennis balls, bound to thick stems
in a yard so foreign it might as well
have been the moon, she can't abide

her marriage. She would prefer
to bake in the oven of sun,
to step on a rattlesnake,
a scorpion—treading the path toward
the hills that surround the arena.

There a million sadness's plague
these forests, and firs blossom
in flames for nothing more
than a chaste wind, an errant match head,
the forked tongue of lightning.

To My God in His Affliction

Scarlet tanagers thread the great wood.
We are told suffering
builds character, told of One who came to wear
a crown of thorns, to die for our manifold sins,
to free the body of its weight.

I watch woodpeckers needle the great wood
behind the house, I see the same gray carpet
under my feet. I walk into the mundane
as into a city whose gates close behind me.
I hear voices

of May birds for whom all is green and blooming.
Rectangular screens keep all
but the smallest gnat
and the largest wolf spider
from entering the house to which I come

chained with hours with no words
to exchange—
no laughter, no children, no toys.
How imagination chafes beneath the mass
of this dull sun meant for another world.

The Sick

A ragged marching band,
they scumble a thicket of notes
making excuses, holding charts,
plaiting the braids of a neighbor,
swallowing pills.
It's a chronic condition,
to be alive and have dreams,
to thirst for greatness
and starve to death.
In their delusions of grandeur
the sick play a winter music.
They sound like birds praising days
when the earth was an organism,
self-sufficient. Like the clear high notes
of flute and violin,
their swollen line picks up stragglers,
dawdlers, followers-on.

In My September

Through glass the trees
are moved by wind,
the saws saw,
and sky's a cornflower blue
the color of loneliness.
Here the month
turns over. At 5 a.m.,
a moon shines hard over
the last dahlias—
a nest of brilliant jewels
I forgot to take,
to pick, to give,
to bury my nose
like a dog in petals
that might have broken
this armor of scales
grown all summer long,
honed now to where
I am made of metal,
ready to tackle another winter.

Mountain Pass, July

The lepers come down
the slow hill of snow
to ask for a piece
of my pain.
They hold out stumps
of hand
and some crutch down
empty ski runs
to reach into this nerve
that stretches
from shoulder to toe
as if it held an aura
made visible by refraction,
a rainbow of sensitivities
honed by war,
and by the severe fastidiousness
with which I turn my neck
to look over my shoulder
and gaze back into years.

Clover

Born small, airless, to grow there
in the garden into an inflammation
of globed heads, nodes with whitish crescents.

Then again, tiny pink to pale flowers
drawn to disturbed sites—
how liquid the past, in retrospect.

Where did luck go?
I visit the past. Inured
to pain it remains the same
kind of mud-brown enclosure
within which horses nuzzle
          the earth.

How did luck begin its famous departure,
from four-leafed to three,
nodules of joy stripped,
barren, inflamed
as by liquid nitrogen against skin.

I visit the past.
An accident, a disease, a missing kidney.
The screen between mother
and child, and blood transferred in utero.
The pain remains the same,
despite scents of mown grass.
Breezeways fill with birdsong.

All is respite and rest
        yet in the nerves
the synapse dances
with disturbance, creeping nodes distill
from mud what thought chances,
catches on.
Obsession in the room,
its labyrinthine game.

My horse—gone, put down due to lameness,
my steady pal, the one who bucked me off
at times, and later returned, head down,
cowering almost
under the glare of sun.

My horse, that speckled gray mare,
white or black
in Revelations, come as if to tell the tears
how, in time future, a cataract
will take the earth—
a foam tsunami.

The yard
goes to seed, tiny, egg-shaped,
shallow notches to bite and hold the light
        in place.

Testimonial

When we lived with the wind it was good to us,
coming and going when we opened the doors

and windows, sighing when we mourned, rustling
through green leaves piled in bough and understory.

We took the wind into our houses and it disturbed
papers and curtains, yet the space remained

as if nothing had been touched, no burglar
bungling an attempt to steal what we'd worked

so hard to keep. This fondness for wind held us
pinned as with centrifugal force—

high-school sweethearts who trauma-bonded,
came apart only when the storm passed. Listen

to what I tell you beneath this canopy
of worry, my frowned-upon husband, my upside-

down smile—are you there? Or is it only
the sound of the fridge turning on in a kitchen.

The heavy breathing of age, the ages
since then, when we lived with the wind.

Fear and Trembling

The Flicker sings *greensickness greensickness*
When you surprise it from a branch
Beside the river. Nietzsche's no longer
Sane, carted off to the asylum with ravings.
The sun doubles as a sun lamp
Beneath which you shower in hot water
As the hour passes, less and less
Your intimate. Quail forage for seeds
In your back, their quick beaks moving
Everywhere at once in hurry scurry,
Comma-shaped crests bobbing
As if royalty visited this wet place.
Leaves! The yellowing of that instinct
For summer, its glimpse of turquoise heaven.
Insects move into memory—you
Must live with ill health now, and autumn.
Because of the fall, obsession and compulsion
Entwine thought. Each new braid proves
You're a master, and on your skin
A rash blooms, angry spots flare. Is it all for this—
The soul's staircase lengthening—the ladder
Leading down?

Milfoil

We remember slime between our toes,
the squishy mud far down
below a roof could be a grave
depending on breath, how long
it could be held, and in that sky-blue place
the flutter kick, light sifting down
to our prison world—we girls—
poor seconds, *do you have ants in your pants,*
as Uncle would say
and yes we were impatient
waiting for dinner to end
so the lake could take us back in its tentacles
close to the surface
like the hair of Ophelia, an acquaintance
closer than the closest friend.

Notes

The epigraph is taken from Jonathan Swift's *Gulliver's Travels*, Unabridged Version, Dover, 1996.

"Short History of the Accident" is accompanied by thoughts on the process of writing, prompted by editors of the journal *Pangyrus* and excerpted here:

> The motivation that led me to write "Short History . . . " is a pedestrian accident that occurred thirty-eight years ago, which is described briefly—the part I remember—in the second stanza. There are other things I recall: being in an ambulance and asking the medic whether I was paralyzed . . . and his answer: "I don't know." In many ways the phrase "I don't know" describes this experience. How can an accident turn one's life upside down? Our bodies remember everything that happens, even if our minds forget.

"The Invalid" is in memory of Gail Laufer, who died at the age of nine in Montreal, in 1963.

"Fragment" refers to Emily Dickinson's famous quote: "Hope is the thing with feathers that perches in the soul—and sings the tunes without the words—and never stops at all."

In "Veils" the term "Padma" refers to the lotus slower Vishnu holds in his fourth arm as a symbol of purity and transcendence.

In "The Sick" the word "scumble" is an art term that means to give a softer effect by applying a very thin coat of opaque paint.

"Fear and Trembling" borrows its title from Kierkegaard.

The lake in "Milfoil" is Lac-MacDonald, Quebec, Canada.

"Taunted," "Below the Snow Line," "Come this way, he said, and I followed him," "Testimonial," "Veils," and "Fear and Trembling" were inspired by the flora and fauna of Cle Elum, Washington.

About the Author

Judith Skillman is a dual citizen of the United States and Canada. She holds a masters in English literature from the University of Maryland and is the author of twenty collections of poetry and a "how to": *Broken Lines—The Art & Craft of Poetry* (Lummox Press). The recipient of awards from the Academy of American Poets and Artist Trust, Skillman's work has appeared in *LitMag, Poetry, Sewanee Review, The Iowa Review, Threepenny Review, Zyzzyva, We Refugees,* and other journals and anthologies.

Ms. Skillman has been a Writer in Residence at the Centrum Foundation in Port Townsend, Washington, and the Hedgebrook Foundation on Whidbey Island. She is the editor, with Linera Lucas, of *When Home Is Not Safe: Writings on Domestic Verbal, Emotional, and Physical Abuse,* from Exposit Books, and a faculty member at Hugo House in Seattle.

Also a visual artist, Ms. Skillman paints expressionist works in oil on canvas. She is interested in feelings engendered by the natural world. Her art has appeared in *Pithead Chapel, Artemis, The Penn Review,* and other journals.

—www.judithskillman.com

SHANTI ARTS

NATURE • ART • SPIRIT

Please visit us online
to browse our entire book catalog,
including poetry collections and fiction,
books on travel, nature, healing, art,
photography, and more.

Also take a look at our highly regarded art
and literary journal, *Still Point Arts Quarterly*,
which may be downloaded for free.

www.shantiarts.com

CPSIA information can be obtained
at www.ICGtesting.com
Printed in the USA
BVHW092324291021
620150BV00005B/155

9 781951 651992